From Grief to Gratitude
after Pet Loss

Healing Messages and Guidance
from Pets in the Afterlife

Marianne Soucy

ISBN-13 978-1541362727

ISBN-10: 1541362721

Table of Contents

Disclaimer:
This book is intended as an informational guide and is not meant to diagnose, treat, or prescribe. For any medical or psychological condition or symptoms, always consult with a qualified physician, or appropriate health care professional. The author or publisher do not take any responsibility for your health or how you choose to use the information contained in this book.

Photos:
The pets' photos are authentic and are taken by their respective owners, and the quality may vary.

Introduction

"I came bearing gratitude, and I leave carrying your love in my heart." ~ Minnie, an angel cat

I am pleased that you have decided to join me for the journey from grief to gratitude after the loss of a beloved pet.

This book is dedicated to my beloved cat Minnie who passed on December 6, 2016 during the writing of this book.

Minnie was all about gratitude – and so is this book.

Like my first book, *Healing Pet* Loss—*Practical Steps for Coping and Comforting Messages from Animals and Spirit Guides*, this book is based on my own experiences and my Sacred Spirit Journeys (a form of shamanic journeying) where I connect with the spirit of animals that are alive, animals in the afterlife, and with spirit guides for healing, guidance, and inspiration.

It was when I lost animals that I loved that I discovered how powerful, comforting, and healing it was to connect with them in the afterlife for healing the grief of the loss. I found the animals to be wise teachers, and the unconditional love they shared so generously when they were alive they continued to share with me along with healing advice even after they had passed.

Since I began connecting with pets in the afterlife, I have done many Sacred Spirit Journeys and brought back many beautiful messages from pets in the afterlife to their grieving human companions. I will share some of those messages in this book as well as healing advice also obtained in my journeys.

In the following, I will give you a few suggestions for how to use this book.

How to use this book

As you begin reading this book, you are entering a sacred space—a sanctuary of peace and loving support where you can heal in your own time and in your own way.

The book will offer you compassionate support and wisdom to guide you through your journey from grief to peace after losing a beloved animal companion.

The journeys in this book are not long intellectual or informational materials, but healing wisdom that is actually more like meditation.

As you read each chapter, do so with your whole being. You are a whole being—physical, emotional, mental, spiritual; so let the wisdom you will receive and the images that will be described to you, become part of you, and join us on the journeys we take.

To get the most out of this book, come back and read the book several times, and the peace you encounter here will be your peace too.

I recommend you combine this book with a daily gratitude practice. Each day, I suggest you read one chapter, and after reading that chapter, write down in a journal or notebook your answer to the action steps and questions at the end of that chapter.

Chapter 1
Getting Started

As described in the previous chapter, the framework of this book is gratitude.

Why is the practice of gratitude so powerful in healing after pet loss – and in life?

Let us look a little more into that.

Feeling gratitude is allowing yourself to open your heart, and thereby also to feel sensitive and vulnerable. However, if you close off your heart, you close it off to the joy as well, and as you know if you are in grief, the pain of the loss will sneak in anyway.

Gratitude is actually a way of building strength, for as you practice gratitude, you heal the past by embracing and acknowledging it fully. You center fully in the present by becoming aware in your life right here, right now, and gratitude enables you to dream and to see a way forward.

Gratitude centers you in your heart and helps you interact with others with more compassion. It also brings you healing, for as you allow yourself to express gratitude, it becomes easier for you to let go of worries, fear, and other thoughts and feelings that prevent you from experiencing peace, joy, and harmony.

You have the best teacher: your animal companion. Animals live in the present moment, and gratitude comes to them so easily. Look to animals for learning how to heal, how to live, and how to grow.

If your pet is alive, you have your teacher with you each day; if your pet has passed, the practice of gratitude can help you heal your grief and reconnect you with your pet in the afterlife.

Action step

Find a quiet moment and sit with your eyes closed. Become present where you are, allowing your body and your mind to slowly calm down in its own time.

After you have been sitting for a little while, focus on your breath going in and out of your body. Do not interfere or control your breath, just let it be as it is.

Then focus on gratitude as you breathe in, and focus on love as you breathe out.

Breathe in gratitude.

Breathe out love.

Do this for a little while.

End this little meditation by becoming present in your body and in the place you are. Open your eyes and look around, extending your awareness to your surroundings.

You are now ready to continue with your day from a place of peace, balance, and gratitude.

Chapter 2
How To Move From Grief To Gratitude After Pet Loss

We begin with a Sacred Spirit Journey where we receive insights on how to move from grief to gratitude after the loss of a beloved pet.

I begin the journey by becoming present where I am, listening to all the sounds as part of these preparations. I notice that nearby someone is listening to loud music, and at first it disturbs me; then, I try not to judge but instead simply allow it to be there, and I listen to all the sounds at the same time without judging or labeling.

I then find myself by the sea in a place I often travel to in my Sacred Spirit Journeys. My spirit guide is there. The sea has high waves. That is rare in my journeys.

"That's part of your teaching today," my spirit guide says, smiling. He continues: *"Like with the sounds, the trick is to allow it all to be there—without judging, without hanging on to any one sound, feeling, or whatever it is. Allow what is there to be there.*

Like the waves come and go, so do the emotions. Sometimes you feel joy, and at other times deep grief. It is when you resist whatever feelings you have that they tend to get worse or you may find yourself stuck in the pain.

If you are struggling with the grief after the loss of a beloved pet, the first step is to acknowledge whatever feelings you have. When you allow them, and don't resist or hold on, you also allow them to shift from grief to gratitude.

One moment you may find yourself hurting from the sorrow of your loss and the next moment you may find yourself smiling, feeling joy by remembering a fond or fun memory of your pet. Allow the grief and the joy to go hand in hand, and let the practice of gratitude be your guide back to peace.

A daily practice of gratitude helps you remember the good times in the midst of your grief. It helps you become present in the Now, and it helps you envision a life moving forward—not with the focus on your pet not being with you in their physical form, but with the knowledge and feeling of your pet's love in your heart and a gratitude for all they gave you and all they were.

Whatever you had together with your pet, no one can take away—and whatever your pet gave you and what they were, they still are.

The gift of love your pet gave you is still with you. Just look inside your heart. The feeling of love transcends time and space. The feeling of love connects you with your pet, even now when they have passed.

Start with the practice of allowing, of not hanging on or resisting, and with a daily gratitude practice.

Blessings and love."

As my spirit guide stops talking, I look around and notice the sea is now calm; the sun is shining and everything looks magical, beautiful, and full of light.

I take the image and feeling of this with me to keep in my heart as I go about my day, and to give as a gift to you now, bringing light into the darkness, and healing love to your broken heart.

Action step

Gratitude is not just a state or feeling we would like to achieve, but it is also a practice.

When we are deep in grief after the loss of a loved one, the practice of gratitude can be a way for us to slowly return to and be okay with the present moment. It can help us experience, that in spite of our great loss, there is still much beauty, love, and kindness available to us.

Gratitude can be a path through the grief, one step at a time. That is where a simple daily practice of gratitude over time can make a big difference. It will help you center in and be present in the Now, which is the best place to get peace and to connect with a beloved pet in the afterlife; this is a message and healing advice that has come up very often in my connections with pets in the afterlife.

If you do not already have a daily gratitude practice, I highly recommend you start today.

I will be sharing different ways of practicing gratitude throughout this book. Dedicate a journal or a notebook to your daily gratitude practice.

Each morning write down three things you are grateful for.

While you are reading this book, you can do your gratitude practice in connection with your reading of each chapter.

Chapter 3
A Message Of Gratitude From An Angel Dog

Very often, it is our animals in the afterlife that can best provide us with the comfort and guidance that we need to heal after the loss of our beloved animal friends.

I experienced that after I lost animals that were close to my heart, and I have seen it countless times with people that came to me looking for comfort after losing their best friend and companion.

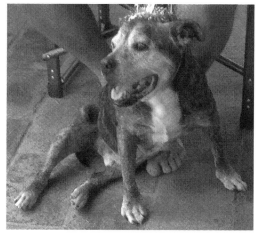

In this chapter, I will share a Sacred Spirit Journey with a message from the angel dog, Jack, to his grieving human companion, Shirley Baker. It is a message that brings comfort, healing, and inspiration not only to Jack's loved ones, but to the rest of us as well. I find myself returning often to this precious dog and his beautiful message.

As I begin the Sacred Spirit Journey to connect with Shirley's angel dog, Jack, I find myself in a place of light.

I notice that Jack is standing by my feet, sniffing and checking me out. He then sits up and looks up at me with joy and openness.

Marianne: "Hi Jack. It's good to see you."

Jack:

"I'm glad you came. I have wanted to bring my messages and my love to Shirley and the rest of the family.

Shirley is especially struggling with the loss, because she had to take the courageous but also compassionate decision to help me get peace. It was my time to go, and I appreciate the loving care you [Shirley] showed me in the end as well as all through my life.

I came into their lives to teach the lesson of unconditional love and of seeing the light in everyone.

I am a reminder to let go of judgments or preconceived ideas, and instead to connect with those you meet on your path through life with openness, love, and in the spirit of joy.

During my life, I spread joy, and as I continue my soul's journey in spirit, my memories will continue to bring joy to the ones that loved me, and my light will shine from beyond as strong as when I was alive.

A light like mine cannot be extinguished. Let my light, love, and teachings rest in your heart and guide you as you continue your own life journey.

My life was lived in gratitude. Let gratitude be a way for you to let go of the pain and a way to connect with my light and me.

Know that I am fine now.

Know that my heart is now also at ease as I know you are receiving my message.

Your heart was open to me, and I know your heart will be open to experiencing my light in your heart once you begin to let go of the guilt and pain you feel.

Take whatever time you need to grieve, and do not let the pain frighten you. Notice the love and gratitude behind the pain. Remember all the fond memories that are buried in your heart. Let the joy of those memories become part of your life again, and share that joy with others who need it. Many have not been blessed with a loving relationship like the one we had.

I honor and bless you all, and send you my loving light now and always. All is well."

Jack stops talking, and as he looks at me his face and his eyes are practically beaming with so much love and light coming from him. He is truly shining his soul's light; what a model and example for us all.

Marianne: "Thank you so much, Jack. I will be honored to pass on your message. Anything else?"

Jack: *"Just this: Don't forget the joy."*

Jack has a glint in his eyes and is full of love, light, and joy as he says goodbye.

I wave goodbye to him, thank my spirit guide, and end the journey.

Action step

Today, write down a fond memory of your pet for which you are grateful.

Chapter 4
Perspectives On Death

Death is a tough subject that we are forced to deal with when our beloved animal companion passes. It turns our life upside down.

In this chapter, I will share insights about death I received during one of my Sacred Spirit Journeys.

When it comes to death, there are two perspectives you can take. On the one hand, you are a physical being; the job for you on a physical level is to be here in your physical body fully. This reality as you experience it is real to you, real and tangible. On that level, love is real and pain is real. There is birth, and there is death. There is a physical body. All those experiences are real to you, but they are not who you are. There is a difference.

When you lose a pet, your loss is very real too; there IS a physical death, and the body of your loved one IS no more. That loss to you is real, painful, and it is okay to grieve that loss.

Then there is the other perspective: the one that while you live in and 'inhabit' your body, you are not just your body; you are so much more than that. Both you and your animal friend also exist on a soul or spirit level.

The essence of who you are is not the body. You can see it when someone has just died. You see their dead body, but you also experience and feel that the essence of who that person or animal was is not there anymore.

That is where the difficult part for most people comes in—connecting with the spirit or soul of the loved one. Because you cannot usually see, feel, or touch it on a physical level, you feel that your loved one is gone and there is nothing more.

When you surrender to the present moment, and allow everything to be as it is, you will feel the pain and grief of the loss of your loved one as they are not physically with you anymore. However, in the peace of the present moment, when you go within your heart, you can experience the happy memories, the love, and everything else you shared with and learned from your animal friend.

Allow yourself to move into a place of gratitude for what was, and for being blessed with sharing your life with this wonderful animal friend of yours. Allow yourself to feel thankful for being able to give—and receive—so much love, and for all the memories you created together.

You have the pain of the loss, but hand in hand with that pain, you also have your continued love for your animal friend, as well as your gratitude.

If you look at yourself and your life before and after you met your animal friend, you will see that you are not the same person. You have grown, your heart has opened, and your awareness has been raised to a higher level because of the purity of the unconditional love you shared.

Therefore, in that respect, your animal friend lives on in who you have become.

Honor and acknowledge that. Celebrate that. Celebrate your love.

Action steps

First, write down three things for which you are grateful. Then follow the action steps below.

1) Allow yourself to grieve. Acknowledge the feelings you have. Express your feelings, perhaps in a letter to your pet, through art, or in another way.

2) Celebrate the life of your animal friend and the love you shared. Express your appreciation and gratitude.

You can also combine all this in a memorial ceremony for your animal friend. It does not have to be complicated or elaborate.

Consider how you can create your own memorial ceremony for your animal companion that includes expressing your feelings of grief, but also gratitude and appreciation.

(See also Chapter 7: A simple way of connecting with a pet in the afterlife)

Chapter 5
An Angel Dog's Healing Message

In this chapter, we will hear a message from Trixie, an angel dog who died suddenly. May her love and healing advice bring you comfort and peace as it did her grieving human companion, Mia Maria.

I connect with Trixie's spirit during one of my Sacred Spirit Journeys. As I begin the journey, I find myself in beautiful ethereal landscape—a place of light. Several of my spirit guides are present and I notice that rose petals are sprinkled around us.

Trixie comes walking towards us, walking on the rose petals put out just for her. I sit down. She comes straight over to me, jumps up on my lap, and looks me in the eyes. My spirit guide brings her some healing water. She drinks and is filled with light.

Trixie says:

"It pains me to see my beloved family suffer with the grief of my sudden loss, and I am glad to have the opportunity to send them a message and all my love.

I will not waste precious time going into the why but instead focus on what is important: to reassure them I am okay and that I love them all with all my heart, now and forever more.

[To her family:] Focus on the gratitude and joy of the time we had together instead of the pain of the sudden loss. That is what I choose to do.

It is important for me to let you know just how grateful I am to have found you and to have been blessed with the time we had together. Many are not as lucky as I was. I got a loving home and experienced so much joy. What more could one ask for?

Let each moment be an opportunity for you to embrace gratitude, for gratitude is the way to peace.

Gratitude helps you remember our fun times together with joy, and gratitude brings you peace in your heart when you realize that the love I gave you will always be yours, just as I carry with me the love you all gave me.

To my fur brother I send my love: you can meet me in your dreams where together we will play."

Then she goes to a family member who is particularly struggling with the pain of her loss. She looks at him with much love. A smile appears on his grieving face as she jumps up to him and says to him, while licking him and sending him joy and love:

"To you I am also deeply grateful, for your heart is big and your love a treasure I will keep. With a heart that has opened to love, grief will

also find a way in. Allow the grief to be there and let it go hand in hand with your love for me, for one does not exclude the other. The grief is an expression of your love. Allow yourself to grieve, in your own way, in your own time. Seek out those who understand and support.

Take extra care of your grieving heart in the time to come but know that all will be well. There is no blame, and no guilt is needed. Only love. Love and gratitude.

When we met, there was love. Remember that love now, and let not the grief cloud your mind or close your heart. Whenever you need me, I am near. Trust your heart, for it is not just broken. When you look behind the grief and the pain, see the light I left behind.

I will be around and light up the way and the life for you all—my family. Much love to you all, now and forever."

Before they say goodbye, she gives him a ball *"as a reminder to bring joy back into your life,"* and a beautiful pink rose *"as a symbol of my love for you all."*

They say goodbye and she walks along the rose-petal covered path while the family member goes home to his family with the gifts from Trixie.

I thank my spirit guides and end the journey.

Action steps

1) What are three things you are grateful for today?

2) Which statements in this journey stand out to you? Highlight or write them down. Perhaps journal on them as to how they relate to you and your life right now.

3) What insights do you get from reading Trixie's journey and message?

Chapter 6
Coping With The Emptiness After Pet Loss

One of the common and very painful challenges many people experience after the loss of a beloved pet is emptiness—the big hole in their heart after the passing of their pet.

I find that the following quote by Charles Dickens expresses so perfectly the feelings after the loss of a dear animal companion:

"And can it be that in a world so full and busy, the loss of one creature makes a void in any heart so wide and deep that nothing but the width and depth of eternity can fill it up!"

I often like to seek insight and guidance by contacting and communicating directly with the pets in the afterlife. In order to get suggestions for dealing with the feeling of emptiness after pet loss, I met my angel cat Pittiput in a Sacred Spirit Journey. In the journey, I met him in a beautiful place filled with light, like high up in the sky—blue, infinite sky, sunlight, and a feeling of space, freedom, peace.

My angel cat Pittiput looks beautiful in the clear light.

Pittiput says:

"An animal companion that shares its life with you becomes not only part of your life, but also part of you as you experience it. When you have a close bond with your animal friend, you cannot imagine life without your pet. So losing that animal companion feels like losing part of yourself.

That is normal, and occurs especially because you mainly look at the physical manifestation of the bond and of the love.

But you and your life are so much more than the physical, and even though getting used to being in the physical world without your beloved animal friend can be very hard, that big hole or emptiness and the pain you feel after a loss will become less; it will also leave you with more peace when you go within and discover the light, love, and connection with your pet that is still there.

It has a lot to do with what you focus your thoughts on. For example, if you only think of the pain of the loss, the emptiness, and what you have lost then you will suffer more. However, if you focus on the joy, the love, and all the fond memories and special moments you had with your pet, the hole you feel will be filled with gratitude. As you look inside, you will find your pet's light and love there. Your life has been forever changed for having your pet in your life. Their love and the lessons they taught you are all part of you now. In the peace of your heart, you will find the light that can guide you as you move forward in your life.

For a specific action step to fill the hole after the loss and ease the pain, practice gratitude. The practice of gratitude will help you shift your perspective from only seeing the loss and the emptiness, to seeing the light your pet left behind and the joy they brought into your life, which is still part of you now.

Make gratitude a daily practice, including things you are grateful for in relation to your pet as well as things in your life now that you are grateful for."

May Pittiput's words bring light, peace, and hope into your life.

Action steps

1) Write down three things you are grateful for.

2) In the text, it is mentioned that you can choose where you put your focus. Today, take a moment and choose what you want to focus on. What word, state, or feeling will be your focus, and what step can you take? For example, if your word is 'peace', how can you bring peace into your life today?

Chapter 7
A Simple Way Of Connecting With A Pet In The Afterlife

In this chapter, I will share an easy way of establishing a connection with a pet in the afterlife. This beautiful advice came during a Sacred Spirit Journey I did to connect with the angel dog Jarra in order to receive a message for his grieving human companion, Amanda. May Jarra's words of love inspire and comfort you.

As I begin the Sacred Spirit Journey to connect with Amanda's angel dog Jarra, I feel I am in darkness, but I am holding a little light.

My spirit guide is with me, also holding a light. Amanda joins us. She is holding a lit candle.

The Goddess of Compassion, another of my spirit guides, comes walking towards us. Jarra is next to her. He sees Amanda and goes to her. Amanda bends down and hugs him.

Amanda is squatting down in front of Jarra as she is hugging him. He places his front legs on her shoulders and licks her face.

Jarra says:

"You're my love and my light. Thanks for brings me the light of your love.

Your love has always been in my heart, and it always will be. Now, with your presence in my spirit life and our souls reconnected in spirit, the light has returned and I am happy.

Just as I always lived in the present moment, let yourself let go of the pain of the past and enter the present where our hearts and souls connect.

To connect with me, light a candle in the dark of night and know in those moments that I am near. The light will create a meeting of our hearts and bring peace to your grieving heart.

Through the light, we will meet, and through the memories of our love and the vision of our continued connection in spirit, we will find peace and joy once more.

Always in your heart, and always by your side.

The strength of your heart and the light of our love will carry us through."

Action step

Create a small ritual or ceremony where you light a candle next to a photo of your angel animal. Take a few minutes to become present and for your thoughts and body to calm down. Look at the photo and the light and express your love and gratitude to your beloved animal friend.

How are you inspired to create your small light ritual or meditation?

Chapter 8
Letting Nature Help You Heal After Pet Loss

In this chapter, you will learn how animals can be our link to nature and to our true self.

Once again, I use a Sacred Spirit Journey to receive insights and guidance. As I begin the journey, I sense my angel cat, Kia, by my side. She says:

"Animals are your connection to nature—to the nature which you are a part of. Most people, however, are disconnected from nature and from their true self.

They think they exist separate from nature, and wonder why they keep having the feeling that something is missing, a feeling of being disconnected and not whole.

Having an animal companion in your life reconnects you with nature, with your own self, and with the stillness—a beingness that is your true nature. Animals have kept the ability to rest in being; the ability to be present in the Now. By living with animals, you move back into the Now, and into the peace that is.

Recognizing the important qualities of your animal companion and finding ways to honor and learn from them is not only a way to honor them, but it is also a powerful way of healing after your loss.

One of the many ways to pay tribute to your animal companion is to honor their connection with nature and to honor the wide variety of living beings that exist on this precious Earth. When you thus reconnect with nature, and its many living beings, practice seeing them all as relations, as part of the One, for we are all connected.

Take a moment and ask yourself how you can connect with or care for nature and its beings where you live. Do it consciously and with purpose: to honor your animal companion. Notice as you give back that you will reconnect with the stillness, beingness, peace, and joy of being in the Now."

Marianne: "Thanks Kia, that sounds good. Could you give some examples?"

Kia says:

"The ways to connect with and care for nature are many, but for an example: you could plant a tree or some flowers, perhaps even flowers that attract or support insects and bees. If you have a garden, think of ways you can honor the life there by using animal and environment friendly methods of caring for your garden. Taking a walk in nature with all your senses open. Walking in awareness and gratitude is also a way of reconnecting and returning to the peace of the Now.

Perhaps your animal companion had a favorite place in nature that they have already showed you. Where did they like to be in nature, and what did they like to do there—rest, play? Let your animal companion be your teacher and show you the way back to peace, joy, and being in the Now."

I thank Kia for her insights and inspiration.

Action steps

1) Write down three things you are grateful for today.

2) Which of Kia's suggestions for connecting with nature can you implement in your life now?

Chapter 9
Dealing With Guilt After Pet Loss

When you have lost a beloved animal companion, one of the most challenging feelings you can experience is the feeling of guilt. It is also a very common feeling after pet loss.

My favorite way to get healing and advice is to turn to my helping spirits in a meditation or Sacred Spirit Journey. The following is what happened when I asked for advice on dealing with guilt after pet loss.

I prepare to connect with my spirit helpers (or guides). I then experience myself standing on the beach at the water's edge. I feel the waves gently touching my feet and moving away.

"Grief is like that too," my spirit helper says, and continues: *"Grief is like the waves, it comes and goes. As you learn to pay attention and allow your grief to be there, you'll notice that grief, and in many cases the guilt, can actually be a portal or opening into gratitude and forgiveness, into remembering and being the love that you shared—the love that you still share and eventually are.*

Make use of the times where grief and guilt wash in over you. Those times are, in fact, a gift—an opportunity for you to go deeper within yourself and discover the place inside where you experience the continued presence and love of your beloved animal friend."

Marianne: "How specifically can people do that?"

Spirit guide:

"The very best way to honor your pet and move from guilt to forgiveness, peace, and love, is to learn from your pet. Use what you have been through as a learning experience. Practice doing so without judging or blaming yourself (or others for that matter).

First, what special gifts or teachings did your pet have for you? From the life you shared with them, what was their biggest teaching to you? How can you implement that in your life now in their honor?

Secondly, if you look the circumstances leading up to or surrounding your pet's death, what can you learn from that? Is there something you can do differently in the future? This part may be easier to go through if you do it with someone who understands, and supports you. Always return to a place of no blame, and to a place of learning. That is how you best honor your pet.

Imagine your pet watching you from the afterlife, and remember the unconditional love they always showed you. You still have access to that love, and you have seen yourself that it is eternal. Don't cut yourself off from the love your pet still has for you—the love that connects you, the love that you are."

Action Step

Take out a notebook or journal and note down what your pet's biggest teaching to you was and contemplate how you can get more of or implement that into your life. For example, if your pet's greatest gift was joy, how can you now bring more joy into your life?

Chapter 10
Dealing With The WHY After Pet Loss

Sometimes when we lose a beloved animal companion, we can get stuck in our grief by keep asking ourselves the question: Why did it happen?

In this chapter, I will share an answer to this question from an angel dog's point of view. The message came to me during a Sacred Spirit Journey I did on behalf of the dog's grieving human companion. I think you will find his words comforting and inspiring. Here is what he said:

"I bring a lesson that is so hard to learn for most people, but which, if learned, would bring so much peace. It is a lesson that nothing in life is certain, and that no matter how much you plan and safeguard yourself, very often things happen and there are no 'reasons'.

Life happens, and for you humans and many of us animals, life is short and must be lived in the present moment to get the most out of it. However, although your existence in this physical body is short or limited, Life as such—your spirit or soul—is beyond those limits. There is a part of you that is eternal, like me here. My physical body is gone, but 'I' am not. My spirit lives on.

Searching for answers and reasons is often one of the biggest causes of guilt and suffering; it keeps so many in pain, and they cannot get closure.

Take a practical approach and ask yourself: Did you do the best you could in the circumstances? Is there anything you could or would do different another time?

You can look into those practical things, and at times doing that may reveal an answer that can lead you to take a different approach next time. You learn from taking action.

However, in my case, where you are stumped by the suddenness of my passing, you understandably are caught up in the search for an answer.

Can you let go of the need to explain? What if I tell you to focus on what is really most important right now: That I am okay; that I love you, and that you are okay?

Don't keep yourself in suffering. I would advise you if you needed to take actions or needed to know something, but so often the reasons are really not so important. Only the love is.

Love is the constant, so return to that, and let not the pain of my sudden inexplicable death prevent you from living and loving fully again, and from trusting that you are doing fine.

Things happen in life that we do not expect, and, as best we can see, 'shouldn't' happen; but, sometimes, that's life. Especially in cases when there IS no why, keep returning to the love. The pain and the doubt keep you in suffering and separation, but returning to love builds a bridge between you and the animal—me! —in the afterlife.

Build that connection, ease your pain in the light of my love, and allow the peace you receive by our renewed connection to inspire and guide you on your path. This way your actions will be taken from a place of clarity and peace and not out of fear and desperation.

I am your loving guide. Allow me to bring you back to peace and joy. Allow my presence to ease your doubts and your pain. There IS no why —there is only love."

Action steps

1) Write down three things you are grateful for today.

2) Take a gratitude walk with an accountability partner where you each list three things you are grateful for.

   That is what my husband and I do. Every evening we go for a short gratitude walk during which we each mention three things we are grateful for.

   How can you create a daily gratitude practice that works for you?

.

Chapter 11
Heart Healing After Pet Loss

In this chapter, I will share a Sacred Spirit Journey with insights for healing your heart after pet loss from one of my compassionate spirit guides.

May these words bring peace and healing to your heart after the loss of your beloved animal companion.

As I begin the journey, I find myself walking on the beach together with one of my spirit guides, with the sea on my left side. The sun is shining, and the air is clear and fresh. The water is vast and glistening in the sun. It's a magical day. My spirit guide says:

"In times of deep sorrow and grief—like when you have lost your beloved animal companion—happiness and joy may be the furthest from your mind. Looking around you, all you see is the emptiness left behind after your beloved animal friend is gone.

Under normal conditions, most people are looking outside themselves for the happiness and joy they seek; for those with an animal companion, the bond as well as the shared time together and love also constitute a big part of the happiness and joy the person experiences. That unconditional love of and from an animal is unique and can often be rare in many people's lives.

After your animal friend is gone, you may find it hard to see the beauty and feel the happiness and joy again, even though the world around you is still filled with beauty. In that case, one thing you can do is to go within, into your heart. Find the inner sanctuary in your heart (like we are here now) and discover there, the love, light, and all the fond memories your animal friend shared with you.

You can even connect with the spirit or essence of your animal friend in that light, as they are part of the light now.

Let yourself rest and heal in that place of light, and rediscover the continued connection with your animal friend. Whatever your doubting mind or others might say, you'll know that in that safe place within your heart's sacred space you can reconnect with your animal friend's light whenever you need. Let that light become part of you and bring it out into the world. Share the light that they were, and that they through you now still are. When you find that light inside, it will be easier for you to see and experience the beauty, light, and love which is also available to you on the outside.

So today, let yourself go within; let your heart heal in the light of the love which is yours. Rest in the sacred space of your heart where you know you're safe, loved, and forever connected with heartstrings to infinity. Nothing you have ever loved can be taken from you. The heart is a portal to that love, and to those you love.

In peace."

Action steps

1) What are three things you are grateful for today? Write them down in your journal or notebook.

Chapter 12
Lessons Your Pet Taught You

Animals are wonderful teachers, and in this Sacred Spirit Journey we learn about some of the lessons our pets teach us.

As I begin the journey, I find myself in a beautiful meadow with pets all around me: happy dogs, cats, birds, and many others. They are all eager to connect and help.

I sit down and feel the Earth beneath me. I place a hand on the ground and feel the Earth, making a strong connection. It brings me fully into the now. My spirit guide, who is with me, says:

"That's one of the things that living with or being around pets does. By interacting with them, they bring you out of your mind and into your body and into the present moment. That, in itself, is profoundly healing. It is also a way to connect with your soul.

You cannot connect with your soul when you are lost in your mind or in your thoughts. To connect with your soul, you need to get back to being in your body and becoming present in each moment—being in the Now.

Another quality pets or animal companions have is that they help you connect with and open your heart. The purity and depth of the love they give makes all the doubts and resistance fall away and enables you to safely open your heart to them, for you know deep inside that their love is true and unconditional.

One of the things that can close or prevent that opening is the grief of the loss of a pet, or the thought of losing that pet. However, that can be and should be dealt with, for the heart-to-heart and soul connection you experience from connecting with a pet is like no other relationship. It is a most beautiful way for you to connect with your own soul, discover your own light and your gifts, and find the inspiration to share those soul gifts of yours with the world where they are so needed.

Pets are particularly good at helping those who have either lost part of or lost contact with their soul, for example through illness, trauma, and the like.

The more aware you are during this process, the more you can assist and benefit from the heart-opening and soul-connecting qualities of your pet.

One thing you can start with today is to express gratitude. Your pets live most of their life with you in eternal gratitude, love, and joy. Just look into their eyes!

How and to whom can you express your gratitude today?"

I thank my spirit guide, and all the animals that showed up today, and end the journey.

As this journey describes, gratitude is a powerful practice. Gratitude helps you:

•   Become present

•   Open your heart

•   Connect with your soul

Gratitude also gives you access to the love and the bond you shared with your pet, which is still accessible to you now through your heart.

Action steps

What are three things you grateful for today?

How and to whom can you express your gratitude today?

Chapter 13
Gratitude As A Way Into Joy

One of the biggest teachings our pets have for us is joy. In the following journey, we get insights on how we can bring more joy into our lives.

As I begin the journey, I find myself in a landscape with grassy hills. I am walking barefoot on the grass. The sea is to my right. I can see, hear, and smell it. I turn right and go towards the sea.

A dog is running around happily on the beach, and I see dolphins jumping out at sea.

Joy is the word and feeling that describes this moment best.

The dog comes to me and says:

"That's right. Joy is what you get when you center in the Now with an attitude of gratitude and appreciation.

Gratitude opens you up to joy—to feeling, being, living, and sharing joy. Joy motivates you to take actions.

Start with gratitude. As you make gratitude a daily practice, at the same time you make centering in the present moment a habit and priority in your life.

As gratitude inspires and opens you to joy, look inside your heart and ask yourself how you can express that joy today.

What are you inspired to do? What brings you joy?

You can use gratitude as a way into joy, and you can use things and activities that bring you joy to center you in the present and open you up to gratitude.

We animals are great teachers of joy & gratitude. We're in your life as a loving reminder of how to live life, and how to create your life."

He then runs off. I thank the dog and my spirit guide and end the journey.

Action steps

1) Write down three things you are grateful for today.

2) Answer these two questions:

    What are you inspired to do?

    What brings you joy?

Chapter 14
An Angel Dog's Message Of Joy

In this chapter, we continue with the lessons of joy from pets in the afterlife. You will hear a healing message of joy from the angel dog, Sophie. The following is an excerpt of the message I received from Sophie for her grieving human companion, Monica Bender.

"I came into their lives to teach them about joy—the kind of joy that comes from no particular reason. Joy needs no reason.

When you enter your heart and let go of all worries, you'll find a little light there—a little bundle of joy. That's me! Although my body is no more, my spirit is shining brightly and ready to bring joy into your lives again.

Allow yourself to grieve, but know and see that together with the grief of the loss, you can still experience the joy from our time together, the fond memories, and my light which still shines on you and in your heart. Nothing or no one can take away the bond and love we had. It's all with you.

So along with acknowledging your grief, also celebrate my life and the love and joy I brought into your life. Let the memories you have of me be a cause for celebration and a way of finding the strength to see forward—not to a life without me, but to a life where I am by your side in spirit, and where all my love and my lessons of joy are part of you as you move forward.

It's not about the length of time we spent together. I came and taught you what I could, and the strength of our bond allowed my joy and love to leave you changed—filled with love, joy and gratitude.

The purpose of life is to live it fully, and that is what I taught you. Remember that as you continue on your soul's path.

Each moment is a gift; embrace it as such and return to gratitude every day. Meet each new day with gratitude. Gratitude for what was, for what is, and what is to come.

The everlasting present moment—that's where you'll find me."

Action steps

The practice of becoming present in the Now is also a powerful way of healing after the loss of a pet. It allows you to acknowledge your feelings and the beauty that is all around you. The practice of gratitude is a way of opening up to experiencing your pet's continued presence in your life now. So the prompt for today is:

1) What are three things you are grateful for RIGHT NOW? Write them down in your journal or notebook.

Chapter 15
Just For Today…

As you have seen throughout this book, the practice of gratitude is a powerful tool for helping you cope with and heal after the loss of a beloved animal companion. In this chapter, I will share a technique (or rather a perspective) you can use to move from grief to gratitude and open up to peace and joy in the midst of your grief.

Nature is a trusted companion on our healing journey, and today, let us once again turn to nature.

I suggest that you go out in nature, or simply look out of your window at the sky as dawn breaks in all its beauty. As you watch that sunrise, let your pain and grief still be there—don't push it away—but simply shift your focus to the beauty of the sunrise you have before you.

Take your time to really become present in this moment.

As you allow yourself to open up to the beauty of the sunrise, you may experience a feeling of awe, and of gratitude.

Hold that feeling of awe and gratitude in your heart while you think of your animal companion that has passed. Then, consciously shift your perspective or make the intention, that as long as you are alive, you will experience the beauty for both of you, as it is so beautifully stated in the quote below.

"As long as I can I will look at this world for both of us. As long as I can I will laugh with the birds, I will sing with the flowers, I will pray to the stars, for both of us". ~ Author unknown

Our animals are such wonderful teachers. As you work on finding your way through the grief and back to gratitude, honor your animal friend by learning from their life and all their wonderful qualities.

Allow your animal companion to help you learn to live life fully. That's what animals are so good at. That's one of the reasons they bring us so much joy.

Why not try this?

Just for today, I'll be grateful for both of us, grateful for a new day, grateful for the beauty I see, and the beauty I carry in my heart of the memories of you.

Just take one day at a time.

Action steps

1) What are three things you are grateful for today? Write them down in your journal.

2) Gratitude Tip

   Create a gratitude board on Pinterest – make your own gratitude images and put up and repin other peoples' images.

   If you are not on Pinterest, you can sign up free at https://www.Pinterest.com.

You can see the Healing Pet Loss Gratitude board on Pinterest:

https://www.pinterest.com/healingpetloss/gratitude

And see also my Give Your Dream Wings gratitude board:

https://www.pinterest.com/shamancoach/gratitude

And while you are visiting Healing Pet Loss on Pinterest, you may want to check out some of my pet loss boards as well.

Chapter 16
Minnie's Message Of Gratitude

I will end with a message of gratitude from my angel cat Minnie who passed on December 6, 2016. The following is an excerpt of a message I received from her about a month before her passing:

> *"... Keep practicing seeing me as the light I am. See the essence of me. Hold that vision for me and for you. That will bring you peace.*
>
> *In gratitude I came to you, in gratitude I have lived with you, and in deep gratitude I pass to where I came from.*
>
> *Meet me in your heart each time you practice gratitude and know that I am near.*
>
> *Always will I love you and bless you.*
>
> *Take good care of yourself and the others.*
>
> *Peace."*
>
> *~ Minnie, an angel cat*

Chapter 17
Resources For Healing Pet Loss

For further pet loss support, and to access the healing pet loss resources mentioned in this book, visit:

http://healingpetloss.com/gratitude-book-resources/

The resources will give you tips, inspiration, and exercises for connecting with your pet in the afterlife, healing your heart, and finding peace after pet loss.

In this book you have seen several examples of the Sacred Spirit Journeys I have done for clients and brought back messages from their pets in the afterlife. On the Healing Pet Loss website you can learn how you can receive a message from *your* pet in the afterlife.

I also invite you to connect with Healing Pet Loss on Facebook:

https://www.facebook.com/healingpetloss

On Instagram, you can find me at:

https://www.instagram.com/healingpetloss

https://www.instagram.com/giveyourdreamwings

About The Author

Marianne Soucy is a bestselling author and coach, host of the Healing Pet Loss Podcast, and a shamanic practitioner. An important part of her work is the healing, wisdom, empowerment, and guidance she receives from animals and spirit guides through her Sacred Spirit Journeys. Many of the beautiful messages she has received  in those journeys can be found in her books and on her websites.

At HealingPetLoss.com, Marianne helps grieving pet owners and connects them with their beloved pets in the afterlife.

At GiveYourDreamWings.com, Marianne provides spiritual and practical guidance to help clients become grounded, centered, and connected to soul and spirit, and create the life their heart is guiding them to live and their soul is yearning for.

Books

Healing Pet Loss—Practical Steps for Coping and Comforting Messages from Animals and Spirit Guides (Kindle and paperback)

From Grief to Gratitude after Pet Loss — Healing Messages and Guidance from Pets in the Afterlife

Notes

This page can be used for your own personal notes.